# Brutus
Voltaire
Translation by William F. Fleming

Start Publishing PD LLC
Copyright © 2024 by Start Publishing PD LLC

All rights reserved, including the right to reproduce this book or portions thereof in any form whatsoever.

Start Publishing PD is a registered trademark of Start Publishing PD LLC
Manufactured in the United States of America

Cover art: Shutterstock/Taisiya Kozorez

Cover design: Jennifer Do

10 9 8 7 6 5 4 3 2 1

ISBN 979-8-8809-0276-7

# Contents

Dramatis Personæ................................................. 3
Act I. ............................................................ 4
Act II. ........................................................... 13
Act III. .......................................................... 21
Act IV. ........................................................... 31
Act V. ............................................................ 38

# Dramatis Personæ

Junius Brutus, Consuls.
Valerius Publicola. Consuls.
Titus, Son of Brutus.
Tullia, Daughter of Tarquin.
Algina, Confidante of Tullia.
Aruns, Ambassador from Porsenna.
Messala, Friend of Titus.
Proculus, A military Tribune.
Albinus, Confidant of Aruns.
Senators. Lictors.

This tragedy was produced in 1730. It marks Voltaire's spirit of daring in treating a subject from which Shakespeare shrank as, perhaps, too painful for representation. When revived during the Revolution it was enthusiastically applauded.

# ACT I.

SCENE I.

Rome, Brutus in the Senate.

The scene represents part of the house appointed for the consuls on the Tarpeian mount: at a distance is seen the temple of the capitol. The senators are assembled between the temple and the house, before the altar of Mars: the two consuls, Brutus and Valerius Publicola preside; the senators ranged in a semicircle, behind them the lictors with their fasces.

**Brutus**: At length, my noble friends, Rome's honored senate, The scourge of tyrants, you who own no kings But Numa's gods, your virtues, and your laws, Our foe begins to know us: this proud Tuscan, The fierce Porsenna, Tarquin's boasted friend, Pleased to protect a tyrant like himself; He who o'er Tiber's banks hath spread his hosts, And borne his head so loftily, now speaks In lowlier terms, respects the senate's power, And dreads the sons of freedom and of Rome: This day he comes, by his ambassador, To treat of peace, and Aruns, sent by him, Demands an audience: he attends even now Your orders in the temple: you'll determine Or to refuse or to admit him to us.

**Valerius Publicola**: Whate'er his errand be, let him be sent Back to his king; imperial Rome should never Treat with her foes till she has conquered them: Thy valiant son, the avenger of his country, Has twice repulsed Etruria's haughty monarch, And much we owe to his victorious arm: But this is not enough; Rome, still besieged, Sees with a jealous eye the tyrant's friends: Let Tarquin yield to our decrees; the laws Doomed him to exile; let him leave the realm, And purge the state of royal villainy; Perhaps we then may listen to his prayers. But this new embassy, it seems, has caught Your easy faith: can you not see that Tarquin, Who could not conquer, thinks he may deceive you. I never loved these king's ambassadors, The worst of foes beneath the mask of friendship; Who only bear an honorable title, And come to cheat us with impunity; Armed with state-cunning, or elate with pride, Commissioned to insult us, or betray. Listen not, Rome, to their deluding tongues; Stranger to art, thy business is, to fight; Conquer the foes that murmur at thy glory, Punish the pride of kings, or fall thyself; Such be thy treaties.

**Brutus**: Rome already knows How much I prize her safety and her freedom; The same my spirit, and the same my purpose, I differ in opinion from Valerius; And must confess, this first great homage paid The citizens of Rome, to me is grateful. I would accustom the despotic power Of princes on an easy level first To treat with our renowned commonweal, Till heaven shall crown our arms with victory, And make them subjects; then, Publicola, As such we'll use them: meantime, Aruns comes, Doubtless to mark the state of Rome, to count Her treasures, and observe her growing power, And therefore would I have him be admitted; Would have him know us fully: a king's slave Shall look on men; the novelty may please him: Let him at leisure cast his eyes o'er Rome, Let him behold her in your patriot breasts, You are her best defence; let him revere The God who calls us hither; let him see The senate, hear and tremble.

**Valerius Publicola**: I submit; [The senators rise and come forward to give their votes.] The general voice is yours: Rome and her Brutus Must be obeyed: for me, I disapprove it: Lictors, attend, and introduce him to us: Never may Rome repent of this! [To Brutus.] On thee Our eyes are fixed; on Brutus, who first broke Our chains; let freedom use a father's voice, And speak by thee.

SCENE II.

The Senate, Aruns, Albinus, Attendants.

[Aruns enters, preceded by two lictors, with Albinus, his friend; he passes by the consuls and senate, salutes them, and sits down on a seat prepared for him towards the front of the stage.]

**Aruns**: With pleasure I behold This great assembly, Rome's illustrious senate, And her sage consuls, famed for truth and justice, Which ne'er till now suffered reproach or blame: I know your deeds, and I admire your virtues; Unlike the wild licentious multitude, The vulgar crowd, whom party rage or joins Or disunites, who love and hate by turns, They know not why, taught in one changeful hour To boast or beg, to rail or to obey; Whose rashness—

**Brutus**: Stop, and learn with more respect To treat the citizens of Rome; for know, It is the senate's glory and her praise To represent that brave and virtuous people Whom thou hast thus reviled: for ourselves, Let us not hear the voice of flattery; It is the poison of Etrurian courts, But ne'er has tainted yet a Roman senate. On with thy message.

**Aruns**: Little doth the pride Of Rome affect me; but I own I feel For her misfortunes, and would plead her cause With filial love: you see the gathering storm Hangs o'er your heads, and threatens sure destruction: In vain hath Titus striven to save his country; With pity I behold that noble youth, Whose ardent courage labors to support Expiring Rome, and make her fall more glorious: His victories cost you dear; they thin your ramparts, And weaken your small force: no longer then Refuse a peace so needful to your safety. The senate bears a father's love to Rome, So does Porsenna to the hapless kings Whom you oppress: but tell me, you who judge Depending monarchs, you who thus determine The rights of all mankind, was it not here, Even at these altars, at this capitol, You called the gods to witness your allegiance, And bound your faith to your acknowledged king, To Tarquin? Say, what power has broken the tie? Who snatched the diadem from Tarquin's head? Who can acquit you of your oaths?

**Brutus**: Himself: Talk not of ties dissolved by guilt, of gods Whom he renounced, or rights which he has lost; We paid him homage, bound ourselves by oath, Oaths of obedience, not of slavery: But since thou bidst us call to our remembrance, The senate making vows for Tarquin's health, And kneeling at his feet, remember thou, That on this sacred spot, this altar here, Before the same attesting gods, that Tarquin Swore to be just; such was the mutual bond Of prince and people, and he gave us back The oath we made, when he forgot his own: Since to Rome's laws no more he pays obedience, Rome is no longer subject to his power, And Tarquin is the rebel, not his people.

**Aruns**: But, grant it true, that power unlimited, And absolute dominion, had misled The unhappy monarch from the paths of duty, Is there a man from human error free? Is there a king without some human weakness? Or if there were, have you a right to punish, You, who were born his subjects; you, whose duty Is to obey? The son doth never arm Against the sire, but with averted eyes Laments his errors, and reveres him still: And not less sacred are the rights of kings; They are our fathers, and the gods alone Their judges: if in anger heaven sometimes Doth send them down, why would you therefore call For heavier chains, and judgments more severe? Why violate the laws you would defend, And only change your empire to destroy it? Taught by misfortune, best of monitors, Tarquin henceforth, more worthy of his throne, Will be more wise and just; the legal bonds Of king and people now may be confirmed By happiest union; public liberty Shall flourish then beneath the awful shade Of regal power.

**Brutus**: Aruns, 'tis now too late: Each nation has its laws, by nature given, Or changed by choice: Etruria, born to serve, Hath ever been the slave of kings or priests; Loves to obey, and, happy in her chains, Would bind them on the necks of all mankind. Greece boasts her freedom; soft Ionia bends Beneath a shameful bondage; Rome had once Her kings, but they were never absolute: Her first great citizen was Romulus, With him his people shared the weight of empire; Numa was governed by the laws he made; Rome fell at last indeed beneath herself, When from Etruria she received her kings, Or from Porsenna; tyranny and vice From your corrupted courts flowed in upon us. Forgive us, gods, the crime of sparing Tarquin So many years! at length his murderous hands, Dyed with our blood, have broke the shameful chain Of our long slavery, and the Roman people Have through misfortune found the road to virtue: Tarquin restores the rights by Tarquin lost, And by his crimes has fixed the public safety: We've taught the Etruscans how to shake off tyrants, And hope they'll profit by the fair example. [The consuls descend towards the altar, and the senate rises.] O Mars, thou god of battles, and of Rome! Thou who dost guard these sacred walls, and fight For thy own people, on thy altar here Deign to accept our solemn oaths, for me And for the senate, for thy worthy sons: If in Rome's bosom there be found a traitor, Who weeps for banished kings, and seeks once more To be a slave, in torments shall he die; His guilty ashes, scattered to the winds, Shall leave behind a more detested name, Even than those tyrant kings which Rome abhors.

**Aruns**: [Stepping towards the altar.] And on this altar, which you thus profane, I call that god to witness, in the name Of him whom you oppress, the injured Tarquin, And great Porsenna, his avenger, here I swear eternal war with you, O Romans! And your posterity— [The senators are going off towards the capitol.] A moment stop Ere you depart, O senators! and hear What I have more to offer: Tarquin's daughter, Must she too fall a sacrifice to Rome? With ignommious fetters will ye bind Her royal hands, to triumph o'er her father, Whose treasures you detain? Ungenerous victors! As if the right of conquest gave them to you: Where are his riches? was it for the spoil You robbed him of his throne? let Brutus speak, And own the plunder.

**Brutus:** Little dost thou know Of Rome, her manners, and her noble nature; But learn, mistaken man, her great protectors, The friends of truth and justice, are grown old In honest poverty; above the pride Of wealth, which they disdain; it is their boast To conquer kings, who love such tinsel greatness. Take back your gold, it is beneath our notice; And for the hateful tyrant's hapless daughter, Though I abhor the wretched race, yet know The senate has consigned her to my care: She hath not tasted here the baneful cup Of flattery, that sweet poison of a court, Or viewed the pomp and dangerous luxury Of Tarquin's palace: little did her youth Profit by them; but all that to her age And sex was due, all her misfortunes claimed, She hath received: let her return this day To Tarquin; Brutus yields her back with joy: Naught should the tyrant have within these walls But Rome's fixed hatred, and the wrath of heaven: You have a day to carry off your treasures, That must suffice: meantime, the sacred rights Of hospitality await thee here; Beneath my roof thou mayest remain in safety: The senate thus by me decrees: bear thou Our answer to Porsenna, and then tell Proud Tarquin, you have seen a Roman senate. [Turning to the senators.] Let us, my friends, adorn the capitol With laurel wreaths, that round the brows of Titus Have spread their noble shade; the arrows too, And bloody ensigns, his victorious hand Hath wrested from the Etruscans: ever thus, From age to age, may the successful race Of Brutus still defend their much loved country: Thus, O ye gods, may you protect us ever; Guide the son's arm, and bless the father's councils!

## SCENE III.

Aruns, Albinus.

[Supposed to have retired from the hall of audience into an apartment of Brutus' house.]

**Aruns:** Didst thou observe the fierce unbending spirit Of this proud senate, which believes itself Invincible? and so perhaps it might be, Were Rome at leisure to confirm her sons In valor and in wisdom: liberty, That liberty, my friend, which all adore, And I admire, though I would wrest it from them, Inspires the heart of man with nobler courage Than nature gives, and warmth almost divine. Beneath the Tarquin's yoke, a slavish court Enfeebled their corrupted hearts, and spoiled Their active valor; whilst their tyrant kings, Busied in conquering their own subjects, left Our happier Etruscans in the arms of peace; But if the senate should awake their virtues, If Rome is free, Italia soon must fall: These lions, whom their keepers made so gentle, Will find their strength again, and rush upon us; Let us then stop this rapid stream of woes, Even at its source, and free a sinking world From slavery; let us bind these haughty Romans Even with the chains which they would throw on us, And all mankind.—But will Messala come, May I expect him here? and will he dare—

**Albinus**: My Lord, he will attend you; every minute We look for him; and Titus is our friend.

**Aruns**: Have you conferred; may I depend on him?

**Albinus**: Messala, if I err not, means to change His own estate, rather than that of Rome; As firm and fearless as if honor guided, And patriot love inspired him; ever secret, And master of himself; no passions move No rage disturbs him; in his height of zeal Calm and unruffled.

**Aruns**: Such he seemed to me When first I saw him at the court of Tarquin; His letters since—but, see, he comes.

## SCENE IV.

Aruns, Messala, Albinus.

**Aruns**: Messala, Thou generous friend of an unhappy master, Will neither Tarquin's nor Porsenna's gold Shake the firm faith of these rough senators? Will neither fear, nor hope, nor pleasure bend Their stubborn hearts? These fierce patrician chiefs. That judge mankind, are they without or vice Or passion? is there aught that's mortal in them?

**Messala**: Their boasts are mighty, but their false pretence To justice, and the fierce austerity Of their proud hearts, are nothing but the thirst Of empire; their pride treads on diadems; Yet whilst they break one chain, they forge another. These great avengers of our liberty, Armed to defend it, are its worst oppressors: Beneath the name of patrons they assume The part of monarchs; Rome but changed her fetters, And for one king hath found a hundred tyrants.

**Aruns**: Is there amongst your citizens a man Honest enough to hate such shameful bondage?

**Messala**: Few, very few, yet feel their miseries: Their spirits, still elate with this new change, Are mad with joy: the meanest wretch among them, Because he helped to pull down monarchy, Assumes its pride, and thinks himself a king: But I've already told you I have friends, Who with reluctance bend to this new yoke; Who look with scorn on a deluded people, And stem the torrent with unshaken firmness; Good men and true, whose hands and hearts were made To change the state of kingdoms, or destroy them.

**Aruns**: What may I hope from these brave Romans? say, Will they serve Tarquin?

**Messala**: They'll do anything; Their lives are thine; but think not, like blind vassals, They will obey a base ungrateful master: They boast no wild enthusiastic zeal, To fall the victims of despotic power, Or madly rush on death to save a tyrant, Who will not know them. Tarquin promises Most nobly, but when he shall be their master, Perhaps he then may fear, perhaps forget them. I know the great too well: in their misfortunes No friends so warm; but in prosperity, Ungrateful oft, they change to bitterest foes: We are the servile tools of their ambition; When useless, thrown aside with proud disdain, Or broke without remorse when we grow dangerous. Our friends expect conditions shall be made; On certain terms you may depend upon them: They only ask a brave and worthy leader To please their fickle taste; a man well known, And well respected; one who may have power To force the king to keep his plighted faith If we succeed; and if we fail, endued With manly courage to avenge our cause.

**Aruns**: You wrote me word the haughty Titus—

**Messala**: Titus Is Rome's support, the son of Brutus; yet—

**Aruns**: How does he brook the senate's base reward For all his services? he saved the city, And merited the consulship, which they, I find, refuse him.

**Messala**: And he murmurs at it. I know his proud and fiery soul is full Of the base injury: for his noble deeds, Naught has he gained but a vain empty triumph; A fleeting shadow of unreal bliss: I am no stranger to his throbbing heart, And strength of passion; in the paths of glory So lately entered, 'twere an easy task To turn his steps aside; for fiery youth Is easily betrayed: and yet what bars To our design! a consul, and a father; His hate of kings; Rome pleading for her safety; The dread of shame, and all his triumphs past. But I have stole into his heart, and know The secret poison that inflames his soul: He sighs for Tullia.

**Aruns**: Ha! for Tullia?

**Messala**: Yes: Scarce could I draw the secret from his breast; He blushed himself at the discovery, Ashamed to own his love; for midst the tumult Of jarring passions, still his zeal prevails For liberty.

**Aruns**: Thus on a single heart, And its unequal movements, must depend, Spite of myself, the fate of Rome: but hence, Albinus, and prepare for Tarquin's tent. [Turning to Messala.] We'll to the princess: I have gained some knowledge, By long experience, of the human heart: I'll try to read her soul; perhaps her hands May weave a net to catch this Roman senate.

# ACT II.

SCENE I.

The scene represents an apartment in the palace of the consuls.

Titus, Messala.

**Messala**: No: 'tis unkind; it hurts my tender friendship: He who but half unveils his secrets, tells Too little or too much: dost thou suspect me?

**Titus**: Do not reproach me; my whole heart is thine.

**Messala**: Thou who so lately didst with me detest The rigorous senate, and pour forth thy plaints In anguish; thou who on this faithful bosom Didst shed so many tears, couldst thou conceal Griefs far more bitter, the keen pangs of love? How could ambition quench the rising flame, And blot out every tender sentiment? Dost thou detest the hateful senate more Than thou lovest Tullia?

**Titus**: O! I love with transport, And hate with fury; ever in extreme; It is the native weakness of my soul, Which much I strive to conquer, but in vain.

**Messala**: But why thus rashly tear thy bleeding wounds? Why weep thy injuries, yet disguise thy love?

**Titus**: Spite of those injuries, spite of all my wrongs, Have I not shed my blood for this proud senate? Thou knowest I have, and didst partake my glory; With joy I told thee of my fair success; It showed, methought, a nobleness of soul To fight for the ungrateful, and I felt The pride of conscious virtue: the misfortunes We have o'ercome with pleasure we impart, But few are anxious to reveal their shame.

**Messala**: Where is the shame, the folly, or disgrace: And what should Titus blush at?

**Titus**: At myself: At my fond foolish passion, that o'erpowers My duty.

**Messala:** Are ambition then, and love, Passions unworthy of a noble mind?

**Titus:** Ambition, love, resentment, all possess The soul of Titus, and by turns inflame it: These consul kings despise my youth; deny me My valor's due reward, the price of blood Shed in their cause: then, midst my sorrows, seize All I hold dear, and snatch my Tullia from me. Alas! I had no hope, and yet my heart Grows jealous now: the fire, long pent within, Bursts forth with inextinguishable rage. I thought it had been o'er; she parted from me, And I had almost gained the victory O'er my rebellious passion: but my race Of glory now is run, and heaven has fixed Its period here: Gods! that the son of Brutus, The foe of kings, should ever be the slave Of Tarquin's race! nay, the ungrateful fair Scorns to accept my conquered heart: I'm slighted; Disdained on every side, and shame o'erwhelms me.

**Messala:** May I with freedom speak to thee?

**Titus:** Thou mayest; Thou knowest I ever have revered thy prudence; Speak therefore, tell me all my faults, Messala.

**Messala:** No: I approve thy love, and thy resentment: Shall Titus authorize this tyrant senate, These sons of arrogance? if thou must blush, Blush for thy patience, Titus, not thy love. Are these the poor rewards of all thy valor, Thy constancy, and truth? a hopeless lover. A weak and powerless citizen of Rome, A poor state-victim, by the senate braved, And scorned by Tullia: sure a heart like thine Might find the means to be revenged on both.

**Titus:** Why wilt thou flatter my despairing soul? Thinkest thou I ever could subdue her hate, Or shake her virtue? 'tis impossible: Thou seest the fatal barriers to our love, Which duty and our fathers place between us: But must she go?

**Messala:** This day, my lord.

**Titus:** Indeed! But I will not complain: for heaven is just To her deservings; she was born to reign.

**Messala:** Heaven had perhaps reserved a fairer empire For beauteous Tullia, but for this proud senate, But for this cruel war, nay but for Titus: Forgive me, sir, you know the inheritance She might have claimed; her brother dead, the throne Of Rome had been her portion—but I've gone Too far—and yet, if with my life, O Titus, I could have served thee, if my blood—

**Titus**: No more: My duty calls, and that shall be obeyed: Man may be free, if he resolves to be so: I own, the dangerous passion for a time O'erpowered my reason; but a soldier's heart Braves every danger: love owes all his power To our own weakness.

**Messala**: The ambassador From Etruria is here: this honor, Sir—

**Titus**: O fatal honor! what would he with me? He comes to snatch my Tullia from my sight; Comes to complete the measure of my woes.

SCENE II.

Titus. Aruns.

**Aruns**: After my long and fruitless toils to serve The state of Rome, and her ungrateful senate, Permit me here to pay the homage due To generous courage, and transcendent virtue; Permit me to admire the gallant hero Who saved his country on the brink of ruin: Alas! thou hast deserved a fairer meed, A cause more noble, and another foe; Thy valor merited a better fate: Kings would rejoice, and such I know there are, To trust their empire with an arm like thine, Who would not dread the virtues they admire, Like jealous Rome and her proud senate: O! I cannot bear to see the noble Titus Serving these haughty tyrants; who, the more You have obliged them, hate you more: to them Your merit's a reproach; mean vulgar souls, Born to obey, they lift the oppressive hand Against their great deliverer, and usurp Their sovereign's rights; from thee they should receive Those orders which they give.

**Titus**: I thank you, Sir, For all your cares, your kind regard for Titus, And guess the cause: your subtle policy Would wind me to your secret purposes, And arm my rage against the commonweal; But think not to impose thus on my frankness; My heart is open, and abhors design: The senate have misused me, and I hate them, I ought to hate them; but I'll serve them still: When Rome engages in the common cause, No private quarrels taint the patriot breast; Superior then to party strife, we rush United on against the general foe: Such are my thoughts, and such they ever will be; Thou knowest me now: or call it virtue in me, Or call it partial fondness, what you please, But, born a Roman, I will die for Rome, And love this hard unjust suspicious senate, More than the pomp and splendor of a court Beneath a master, for I am the son Of Brutus, and have graved upon my heart The love of freedom, and the hate of kings.

**Aruns**: But does not Titus soothe his flattered heart With fancied bliss, and visionary charms? I too, my lord, though born within the sway Of regal power, am fond of liberty; You languish for her, yet enjoy her not. Is there on earth, with all your boasted freedom, Aught more despotic than a commonweal? Your laws are tyrants; and their barbarous rigor Deaf to the voice of merit, to applause, To family, and fame, throws down distinction; The senate grind you, and the people scorn; You must affright them, or they will enslave you: A citizen of Rome is ever jealous Or insolent; he is your equal still, Or still your foe, because inferior to you: He cannot bear the lustre of high fortune; Looks with an eye severe on every action; In all the service you have done him, sees Naught but the injury you have power to do; And for the blood which you have shed for him, You'll be repaid at last with—banishment. A court, I own's a dangerous element, And has its storms, but not so frequent; smooth Its current glides, its surface more serene: That boasted native of another soil, Fair liberty, here sheds her sweetest flowers: A king can love, can recompense your service, And mingles happiness with glory; there Cherished beneath the shade of royal favor, Long mayest thou flourish, only serve a master, And be thyself the lord of all beside: The vulgar, ever to their sovereign's will Obedient, still respect and honor those Whom he protects, nay love his very faults: We never tremble at a haughty senate, Or her harsh laws: O! would that, born as thou art, To shine with equal lustre in a court Or in a camp, thou wouldst but taste the charms Of Tarquin's goodness! for he loved thee, Titus, And would have shared his fortunes with thee; then Had the proud senate, prostrate at thy feet—

**Titus**: I've seen the court of Tarquin, and despise it: I know I might have cringed for his protection, Been his first slave, and tyrannized beneath him; But, thanks to heaven, I am not fallen so low: I would be great, but not by meanness rise To grandeur: no, it never was my fate To serve: I'll conquer kings, do thou obey them.

**Aruns**: I must approve thy constancy; but think, My lord, how Tarquin, in thy infant years, Guided thy tender youth: he oft remembers The pleasing office, and but yesterday, Lamenting his lost son, and sad misfortunes, "Titus," said he, "was once my best support, He loved us all, and he alone deserved My kingdom and my daughter."

**Titus**: Ha! his daughter! Ye gods! my Tullia! O unhappy vows!

**Aruns**: Even now I carry her to Tarquin; him Whom thou hast thus deserted, far from thee, And from her country, soon must Tullia go; Liguria's king accepts of her in marriage: Meantime thou, Titus, must obey the senate, Oppress her father, and destroy his kingdom: And may these vaulted roofs, these towers in flame, And this proud capitol in ashes laid, Like funeral torches, shine before your people, To light the Roman senate to its grave. Or serve to grace our happy Tullia's nuptials!

**SCENE III.**

Titus, Messala.

**Titus**: Messala, in what anguish hath he left me! Would Tarquin then have given her to my arms! O cruel fate! and might I thus—O no, Deceitful minister! thou camest to search My foolish heart; alas! he saw too well, Read in my eyes the dear destructive passion, He knows my weakness, and returns to Tarquin To smile at Titus, and insult his love: And might I then have wedded her, possessed That lovely maid, and spent a life of bliss Within her arms, had heaven allotted me So fair a fate! O I am doubly wretched.

**Messala**: Thou mightest be happy; Aruns would assist thee, Trust me, he would, and second thy warm wishes.

**Titus**: No: I must bid adieu to my fond hopes; Rome calls me to the capitol; the people Who raised triumphal arches to my glory, And love me for my labors past, expect me, To take with them the inviolable oath, The solemn pledge of sacred liberty.

**Messala**: Go then, and serve your tyrants.

**Titus**: I will serve them; It is my duty, and I must fulfil it.

**Messala**: And yet you sigh.

**Titus**: 'Tis a hard victory.

**Messala**: And bought too dearly.

**Titus**: Therefore 'tis more glorious. Messala, do not leave me in affliction. [Exit Titus.]

**Messala**: I'll follow him, to sharpen his resentment, And strike the envenomed dagger to his heart.

SCENE IV.

Brutus, Messala.

**Brutus**: Messala, stop; I'd speak with you.

**Messala**: With me?

**Brutus**: With you. A deadly poison late hath spread Its secret venom o'er my house: my son, Tiberius, is with jealous rage inflamed Against his brother; it appears too plain; Whilst Titus burns with most unjust resentment Against the senate: the ambassador, That shrewd Etruscan, has observed their weakness, And doubtless profits by it: he has talked To both: I dread the tongues of subtle statesmen, Grown old in the chicanery of a court: To-morrow he returns: a day's too much To give a traitor, and ofttimes is fatal: Go thou, Messala, tell him he must hence This day: I'll have it so.

**Messala**: 'Tis prudent, Sir, And I obey you.

**Brutus**: But this is not all: My son, the noble Titus, loves thee well; I know the power that sacred friendship hath O'er minds like his; a stranger to distrust Or diffidence, he yields his artless soul To thy experience; and the more his heart Relies on thee, the more may I expect, That, able as thou art to guide his steps, Thou wilt not turn them from the paths of virtue, Or take advantage of his easy youth To taint his guiltless heart with fond ambition.

**Messala**: That was even now the subject of our converse; He strives to imitate his godlike sire; Rome's safety is the object of his care: Blindly he loves his country, and his father.

**Brutus**: And so he ought; but above all, the laws; To them he should be still a faithful slave; Who breaks the laws, can never love his country.

**Messala**: We know his patriot zeal, and both have seen it.

**Brutus**: He did his duty.

**Messala**: Rome had done hers too, If she had honored more so good a son.

**Brutus**: Messala, no: it suited not his age To take the consulship; he had not even The voice of Brutus: trust me, the success Of his ambition would have soon corrupted His noble mind, and the rewards of virtue Had then become hereditary: soon Should we have seen the base unworthy son Of a brave father claim superior rank, Unmerited, in sloth and luxury, As our last Tarquin but too plainly proved. How very seldom they deserve a crown Who're born to wear it! O! preserve us, heaven, From such destructive vile abuse of power, The nurse of folly, and the grave of virtue! If thou indeed dost love my son, (and much I hope thou dost) show him a fairer path To glory; root out from his heart the pride Of false ambition: he who serves the state Is amply recompensed: the son of Brutus Should shine a bright example to the world Of every virtue: he is Rome's support, As such I look upon him; and the more He has already done to serve his country, The more I shall require of him hereafter. Know then by what I wish the love I bear him, Temper the heat of youth; to flatter Titus Were death to him, and injury to Rome.

**Messala**: My lord, I am content to follow Titus, To imitate his valor, not instruct him: I have but little influence o'er your son; But, if he deigns to listen to my counsels, Rome soon will see how much he loves her glory.

**Brutus**: Go then, be careful not to soothe his errors; For I hate tyrants much, but flatterers more. [Exit Brutus

## SCENE V.

**Messala:** [Alone.] There's not a tyrant more detestable, More cruel than thy own relentless soul; But I shall tread perhaps beneath my feet The pride of all thy false insulting virtue: Yes, thou Colossus, raised thus high above us By a vile crowd, the thunder is prepared, Soon shall it fall, and crush thee into ruin.

# ACT III.

SCENE I.

Aruns, Albinus, Messala.

**Aruns**: [A letter in his hand.] At length, my friend, a dawn of fair success Breaks in upon us; thou hast served me nobly, And all is well: this letter, my Albinus, Decides the fate of Tarquin, and of Rome. But, tell me, have you fixed the important hour? Have you watched closely the Quirinal gate? If our conspirators to-night should fail To yield the ramparts up, will your assault Be ready? Is the king well satisfied, Thinkest thou, Albinus, we shall bring him back To Rome subjected, or to Rome in blood?

**Albinus**: My lord, by midnight all will be prepared; Tarquin already reaps the promised harvest; From you, once more, receives the diadem, And owns himself indebted more to Aruns Than to Porsenna.

**Aruns**: Or the envious gods, Foes to our hapless sovereign, must destroy Our fair design, well worthy of their aid; Or by to-morrow's dawn rebellious Rome Shall own a master; Rome perhaps in ashes, Or bathing in her blood. But better is it A king should rule o'er an unhappy people, Who are obedient, than in plenty's lap, O'er a proud nation, who are still perverse And obstinate, because they are too happy. Albinus, I attend the Princess here In secret—Stay, Messala.

SCENE II.

Aruns, Messala.

**Aruns**: Touching Titus, What has thou done? couldst thou prevail on him To serve the cause of Tarquin? couldst thou bind His haughty soul?

**Messala**: No: I presumed too far; He is inflexible: he loves his country, And has too much of Brutus in him; murmurs Against the senate, but still dotes on Tullia: Pride and ambition, love and jealousy, Opened, I thought, a passage to his soul, And gave my arts some promise of success; But, strange infatuation!

liberty Prevailed o'er all: his love is desperate, Yet Rome is stronger even than love: in vain I strove, by slow degrees, to efface the horror Which Rome had taught his foolish heart to feel Even at the name of king; in vain opposed His rooted prejudice; the very mention Of Tarquin fired his soul; he would not hear me, But broke off the discourse: I must have gone Too far, had I persisted.

**Aruns**: Then, Messala, There are no hopes of him.

**Messala**: Much less reluctant I found his brother; one of Brutus' sons, At least is ours.

**Aruns**: Already hast thou gained Tiberius? by what lucky art, Messala—

**Messala**: His own ambition did it all: long time, With jealous eye, hath he beheld the honors Heaped on his brother, that eclipse his own; The wreath of laurel, and the pomp of triumph, The waving ensigns, with the people's love, And Brutus' fondness, lavished all on Titus, Like deepest injuries, sunk into his soul, And helped to fill the poisoned cup of envy; Whilst Titus, void of malice or revenge, Too much superior to be jealous of him, Stretched forth his hand from his triumphal car, As if he wished to give his brother part Of all his glories: I embraced, with joy, The lucky minute; pointed out the paths Of glory; promised, in the name of Tarquin, All the fair honors Rome could give, the throne Alone excepted: I perceived him stagger, And saw him bend, by slow degrees, before me: He's yours, my lord, and longs to speak with you

**Aruns**: Will he deliver the Quirinal gate, Messala?

**Messala**: Titus is commander there, And he alone can give it us: already His virtues have been fatal to our purpose; He is the guardian deity of Rome: The attack is dangerous: without his support Success were doubtful, with it all is certain.

**Aruns**: If he solicited the consulship, Thinkest thou he would refuse the sovereign power The sure reversion of a throne with Tullia?

**Messala**: 'Twere an affront to his exalted virtue To offer him a throne.

**Aruns**: And Tullia with it?

**Messala:** O he adores her; and even loves her more, Because he strives to hate; detests the father, And rages for the daughter; dreads to speak, Yet mourns in silence; seeks her everywhere, Yet shuns her presence, and drinks up his tears In secret anguish: all the rage of love Possesses him; sometimes in storms like these A lucky moment turns the wavering mind. Titus, I know, is turbulent and bold; And, if we gain him, may, perhaps, go further Even than we wish: who knows but fierce ambition May yet rekindle by the torch of love! His heart would glow with pleasure, to behold The trembling senate prostrate at his feet. Yet, let me not deceive you with the hopes, That Titus ever will be ours; once more, However, I shall try his stubborn virtue.

**Aruns:** If still he loves, I shall depend on him: One look of Tullia's, one sweet word from her, Will soften his reluctant heart much more, Than all the arts of Aruns or Messala: For, O, believe me, we must hope for naught From men, but through their weakness and their follies: Titus and Tullia must promote our cause; The one's ambition, and the other's love: These, these, my friend, are the conspirators That best will serve the king: from them I hope Much more than from myself. [Exit Messala.]

### SCENE III.

Tullia, Aruns, Algina.

**Aruns:** This letter, Madam, With orders to deliver it to your hands, I have received from Tarquin.

**Tullia:** Gracious heaven! Preserve my father, and reverse his fate! [She reads.] "The throne of Rome may from its ashes rise, And he who was the conqueror of his king Be his restorer: Titus is a hero, He must defend that sceptre which I wish To share with him. Remember, O my Tullia, That Tarquin gave thee life; remember too, My fate depends on thee; thou mayest refuse Liguria's king: if Titus be thy choice, He's mine; receive him for thy husband." Ha! Read I aright! Titus! impossible! Could Tarquin, could my father, still unmoved In all his sorrows, thus at last relent? How could he know, or whence— [Turning to Messala.] Alas, my lord, 'Tis but to search the secrets of my heart You try me thus: pity a wretched princess, Nor spread your snares for helpless youth like mine.

**Aruns**: Madam, I only mean to obey your father, And serve his honored daughter; for your secrets, In me it were presumption to remove The sacred veil which you have drawn before them; My duty only bids me say, that heaven By you determines to restore our empire.

**Tullia**: And is it possible, that Tullia thus Should be the friend of Tarquin, and the wife Of Titus?

**Aruns**: Doubt it not: that noble hero Already burns to serve the royal race: His generous heart abhors the savage fierceness Of this new commonweal; his pride was hurt By their refusal of his just demand: The work's half done, and thou must finish it. I have not looked into his heart; but sure, If he knows Tullia well, he must adore her: Who could behold, unmoved, a diadem By thee presented, and with thee adorned? Speak to him then, for thou alone hast power To triumph o'er this enemy of kings: No longer let the senate boast of Titus, Their best support, the guardian god of Rome; But be it Tullia's glory to possess The great defender of her father's cause, And crush his foes to ruin.

SCENE IV.

Tullia, Algina.

**Tullia**: Gracious heaven! How much I owe to thy propitious goodness! My tears have moved thee: all is changed; and now Thy justice, smiling on my passion, gives New strength and freedom to the glorious flame. Fly, my Algina, bring him hither: gods! Does he avoid me still, or knows he not His happiness? But stay, perhaps my hopes Are but delusions all: does Titus hate The senate thus? alas! and must I owe That to resentment which is due to love?

**Algina**: I know the senate have offended him; That he's ambitious; that he burns for Tullia.

**Tullia**: Then he'll do all to serve me: fly, Algina, Away, begone. [Exit Algina.] And yet this sudden change Alarms me: O! what anguish racks my heart! Now, love, do thou assist and guide my virtue! My fame, my duty, reason, all command it And shall my father owe his crown to me, Shall Tullia be the chain to bind their friendship; And all Rome's happiness depend on mine? O, when shall I impart to thee, my Titus, The wondrous change we little thought to see,

When shall I hear thy vows, and give thee mine, Without a pain, a sorrow, or a fear? My woes are past; now, Rome, I can forgive thee; If Titus leaves thee, Rome, thou art a slave: If he is mine, proud senate, thou art no more: He loves me; tremble therefore, and obey.

SCENE V.

Titus, Tullia.

**Titus**: May I believe it? wilt thou deign once more To look on this abhorred Roman, long The object of thy hatred, and thy foe?

**Tullia**: The face of things, my lord, is strangely altered; Fate now permits me—but first tell me, Titus, Has Tullia still an interest in thy heart?

**Titus**: Alas! thou canst not doubt thy fatal power; Thou knowest my love, my guilt, and my despair; And holdest a cruel empire o'er a life Which I detest; exhaust your rage upon me; My fate is in your hands.

**Tullia**: Know, mine depends On thee.

**Titus**: On Titus? never can this trembling heart Believe it: am I then no longer hated? Speak on, my Tullia: O, what flattering hope Thus in a moment lifts me to the height Of mortal bliss?

**Tullia**: [Giving him the letter.] Read this, and make thyself, Thy Tullia, and her father happy—Now May I not hope—but wherefore that stern brow And frowning aspect? gods!

**Titus**: Of all mankind Titus is sure the most accursed: blind fate, Bent on my ruin, showed me happiness, Then snatched it from me: to complete my woes, It doomed me to adore, and to destroy thee: I love thee, and have lost thee now forever.

**Tullia**: How, Titus!

**Titus**: Yes; this fatal hour condemns me To shame and horror: to betray or Rome Or Tullia: all that's left to my sad choice Is guilt, or misery.

**Tullia**: What sayest thou, Titus? When with this hand I offer thee a throne; Now when thou knowest my heart, for no longer Will I conceal my virtuous passion for thee; When duty yields a sanction to our love; Alas! I thought this happy day would prove The fairest of my life, and yet the moment When first my fearful heart, without a blush, Might own its passion, is the first that calls For my repentance. Darest thou talk to me Of guilt and misery? Know, thus to serve Ungrateful men against their lawful prince, To scorn my proffered bounties, and oppress me, These are my miseries, Titus, these thy crimes. Mistaken youth, weigh in the even balance What Rome refused, and what she offers thee: Or deal forth laws, or meanly stoop to obey them: Be governed by a rabble, or a king; By Rome, or me: direct him right, ye gods!

**Titus**: [Giving her back the letter.] My choice is made.

**Tullia**: And fearest thou to avow it? Be bold, and speak at once; deserve my pardon, Or merit my revenge: what's thy resolve?

**Titus**: 'Tis to be worthy of thee, of myself, And of my country; to be just, and faithful; 'Tis to adore and imitate thy virtues; It is to lose, O Tullia, yet deserve thee.

**Tullia**: Forever then—

**Titus**: Forgive me, dearest Tullia; Pity my weakness, and forget my love: Pity a heart foe to itself, a heart A thousand times more wretched now than even When thou didst hate me: O! I cannot leave, I cannot follow thee; I cannot live Or with thee or without thee; but will die Rather than see thee given to another.

**Tullia**: My heart's still thine, and I forgive thee, Titus.

**Titus**: If thou dost love me, Tullia, be a Roman; Be more than queen, and love the commonweal: Bring with thee patriot zeal, the love of Rome, And of her sacred laws, be that thy dowry: Henceforth let Brutus be thy father, Rome Thy mother, and her loved avenger, Titus, Thy husband: thus shall Romans yield the palm Of glory to an Etruscan maid, and owe Their freedom to the daughter of a king.

**Tullia**: And wouldst thou wish me to betray—

**Titus:** My soul, Urged to despair, hath lost itself: O no! Treason is horrible in every shape, And most unworthy of thee: well I know A father's rights; his power is absolute, And must not be disputed: well I know That Titus loves thee, that he is distracted.

**Tullia:** Thou knowest what duty is, hear then the voice Of Tullia's father.

**Titus:** And forget my own! Forget my country!

**Tullia:** Canst thou call it thine Without thy Tullia?

**Titus:** We are foes by nature; The laws have laid a cruel duty on us.

**Tullia:** Titus and Tullia foes! how could that word E'er pass thy lips!

**Titus:** Thou knowest my heart belies them.

**Tullia:** Dare then to serve, and if thou lovest, revenge me.

SCENE VI.

Brutus, Aruns, Titus, Tullia, Messala, Albinus, Proculus, Lictors.

**Brutus:** [Addressing himself to Tullia.] Madam, the time is come for your departure; Whilst public tumults shook the commonweal, And the wild tempest howled around us, Rome Could not restore you to your household gods: Tarquin himself, in that disastrous hour, Too busy in the ruin of his people To think on Tullia, ne'er demanded thee. Forgive me if I call thus to remembrance Thy sorrows past: I robbed thee of a father, And meet it is I prove a father to thee: Go, princess, and may justice ever guard The throne which heaven hath called thee to possess! If thou dost hope obedience from thy subjects, Obey the laws, and tremble for thyself, When thou considerest all a sovereign's duty: And if the fatal powers of flattery e'er Should from thy heart unloose the sacred bonds Of justice, think on Rome; remember Tarquin: Let his example be the instructive lesson To future kings, and make the world more happy. Aruns, the senate gives her to thy care; A father and a husband at your hands Expect her. Proculus attends you hence, Far as the sacred gate.

**Titus**: [Apart.] Despair, and horror! I will not suffer it—permit me, sir, [Advancing towards Aruns.] [Brutus and Tullia with their Attendants go out, leaving Aruns and Messala.] Gods! I shall die of grief and shame: but soft, Aruns, I'd speak with you.

**Aruns**: My lord, the time Is short; I follow Brutus, and the princess; Remember, I can put off her departure But for an hour, and after that, my lord, 'Twill be too late to talk with me; within We may confer on Tullia's fate, perhaps On yours. [Exit.]

SCENE VII.

Titus, Messala.

**Messala**: O cruel destiny! to join And then divide us! Were we made, alas! But to be foes! My friend, I beg thee stop The tide of grief and rage.

**Messala**: I weep to see So many virtues and so many charms Rewarded thus: a heart like hers deserved To have been thine, and thine alone.

**Titus**: O no! Titus and Tullia ne'er shall be united.

**Messala**: Wherefore, my lord? what idle scruples rise To thwart your wishes?

**Titus**: The ungenerous laws She has imposed upon me: cruel maid! Must I then serve the tyrants I have conquered, Must I betray the people I had saved? Shall love, whose power I had so long defied, At last subdue me thus? Shall I expose My father to these proud despotic lords! And such a father, such a fair example To all mankind, the guardian of his country, Whom long I followed in the paths of honor, And might perhaps even one day have excelled; Shall Titus fall from such exalted virtue To infamy and vice? detested thought!

**Messala**: Thou art a Roman, rise to nobler views, And be a king; heaven offers thee a throne: Empire and love, and glory, and revenge Await thee: this proud consul, this support Of falling Rome, this idol of the people, If fortune had not crowned him with success, If Titus had not conquered for his father, Had been a rebel: thou hast gained the name Of conqueror, now assume a nobler title; Now be thy country's friend, and give her peace. Restore the happy days, when, blessed with freedom, Not unrestrained by power, our ancestors Weighed in the even scale, and balanced well The prince's honors and the people's right: Rome's hate of kings is not immortal; soon Would it be changed to love if Titus reigned: For monarchy, so oft admired, so oft Detested by us, is the best or worst Of human governments: A tyrant king Will make it dreadful, and a good, divine.

**Titus**: Messala, dost thou know me? Dost thou know I hold thee for a traitor, and myself Almost as guilty for conversing with thee?

**Messala**: Know thou, the honor thou contemnest shall soon Be wrested from thee, and another hand Perform thy office.

**Titus**: Ha! another! who?

**Messala**: Thy brother.

**Titus**: Ay! my brother.

**Messala**: He has given His faith to Tarquin.

**Titus**: Could Tiberius e'er Betray his country?

**Messala**: He will serve his king, And be a friend to Rome: in spite of thee, Tarquin will give his daughter to the man Who shall with warmest zeal defend her father.

**Titus**: Perfidious wretch! thou hast misled my steps. And left me hanging o'er the precipice; Left me the dreadful choice or to accuse My brother, or partake his guilt; but know, Sooner thy blood—

**Messala**: My life is in thy power, Take it this moment; I deserve to die For striving to oblige you: shed the blood Of friend, of mistress, and of brother; lay The breathless victims all before the senate, And for thy virtues ask the consulship: Or let me hence, and tell them all I know, Accuse my fellow-traitors, and myself Begin the sacrifice.

**Titus**: Messala, stop, Or dread my desperate rage.

## SCENE VIII.

Titus, Messala, Albinus.

**Albinus**: The ambassador Would see you now, my lord; he's with the princess.

**Titus**: Yes, I will fly to Tullia: O ye gods Of Rome, ye guardians of my much-loved country! Pierce this corrupted, this ungrateful heart: Had Titus never loved, he had been virtuous: And must I fall a sacrifice to thee, Detested senate! let us hence. [Turning to Messala.] Thou seest, Messala, this proud capitol replete With monuments of Titus' faith.

**Messala**: 'Tis filled By a proud senate.

**Titus**: Ay: I know it well: But hark! I hear the voice of angry heaven, It speaks to me in thunder, and cries, stop, Ungrateful Titus, thou betrayest thy country: No, Rome, no, Brutus, I am still thy son: O'er Titus' head the sun of glory still Hath shed his brightest rays; he never yet Disgraced his noble blood: your victim, gods, Is spotless yet; and if this fatal day Shall doom me to involuntary crimes, If I must yield to fate, let Titus die Whilst he is innocent, and save his country.

# ACT IV.

## SCENE I.

titus, aruns, messala. **Titus**: Urge me no more: I've heard too much already: Shame and despair surround me, but begone, I am resolved: go, leave me to my sorrows, And to my virtue: reason pleads in vain, But Tullia's tears are eloquent indeed: One look from her will more unman my soul Than all your tyrant's threats: but never more Will I behold her; let her go: O heaven!

**Aruns**: I stayed but to oblige you, sir, beyond The time which you so earnestly requested, And which we scarce could gain.

**Titus**: Did I request it?

**Aruns**: You did, my lord, and I in secret hoped A fairer fate would crown your loves; but now 'Tis past; we must not think on't.

**Titus**: Cruel Aruns! Thou hast beheld my shame, and my disgrace, Thou hast seen Titus for a moment doubtful: Thou artful witness of my folly, hence! And tell thy royal masters all my weakness; Tell the proud tyrants, that their conqueror, The son of Brutus, wept before thy face; But tell them too, that, spite of all my tears, Spite of thy eloquence, and Tullia's charms, I yet am free, a conqueror o'er myself: That, still a Roman, I will never yield To Tarquin's blood, but swear eternal war Against the race of her whom I adore.

**Aruns**: Titus, I pity and excuse thy grief; And, far from wishing to oppress thy heart With added sorrows, mix my sighs with thine; Only remember, thou hast killed thy Tullia Farewell, my lord.

**Messala**: O heaven!

## SCENE II.

Titus, Messala.

**Titus**: She must not go: On peril of my life I'll keep her here.

**Messala**: You would not—

**Titus**: No: I'll not betray my country: Rome may divide her from me, but she never Can disunite our fate; I live, and breathe For Tullia only, and for her will die. Messala, haste, have pity on my woes, Gather our troops, assemble all our friends. Spite of the senate I will stop her; say She must remain a hostage here at Rome; I'll do it, Messala.

**Messala**: To what desperate means Doth passion urge you? What will it avail To make this fond avowal of your love?

**Titus**: Go to the senate, and appeal to them, Try if thou canst not soften the proud hearts Of these imperious kings. Messala, tell them The interest of Brutus, of the state— Alas! I rave, 'tis idle, and all in vain.

**Messala**: I see you're hurt, my lord, and I will serve you. I go—

**Titus**: I'll see her: speak to her, Messala, She passes by this way, and I will take My last farewell of her.

**Messala**: You shall.

**Titus**: 'Tis she Now I am lost indeed.

### SCENE III.

Titus, Messala, Tullia, Algina.

**Algina**: Madam, they wait.

**Tullia**: Pity my hard, my cruel fate, Algina; This base ungrateful man still wounds my heart; And Brutus, like a vengeful god, appears To torture us: love, fear and grief, at once Distract my soul: let us begone.

**Titus**: O no! Stay, Tullia, deign at least—

**Tullia:** Barbarian, hence! Thinkest thou with soothing words—

**Titus:** Alas! my Tullia, I only know in this disastrous hour What duty bids me do, not what I would: Reason no longer holds her empire here, For thou hast torn her from me, and usurpest The power supreme o'er this distracted mind: Reign, tyrant, stretch thy cruel power; command Thy vassal; bid thy Titus rush on guilt; Dictate his crimes, and make him wretched; No; Sooner than Titus shall betray his country, Give up his friends, his fellow citizens, Those whom his valor saved to fire and slaughter, Sooner than leave his father to the sword Of Tarquin, know, proud woman—

**Tullia:** Shield me, heaven! Thou pleadest the cause of nature, and her voice Is dear to me as to thyself: thou, Titus, Taughtest me long since to tremble for a father; Brutus is mine; our blood united flows: Canst thou require a fairer pledge than love And truth have given thee: if I stay with thee, I am his daughter, and his hostage here. Canst thou yet doubt? thinkest thou in secret Brutus Would not rejoice to see thee on a throne? He hath not placed indeed a diadem On his own brows, but is he not a king Beneath another name? and one year's reign Perhaps may bring—but these are fruitless reasons. If thou no longer lovest me—one word more, Farewell: I leave, and I adore thee, Titus: Thou weepest, thou tremblest; yet a little time Is left for thee. Speak, tell me, cruel man, What more canst thou desire?

**Titus:** Thy hatred; that Alone remains to make me truly wretched.

**Tullia:** It is too much to bear thy causeless plaints; To hear thee talk of fancied injuries, With idle dreams of visionary ties: Take back thy love, take back thy faithless vows, Worse than thy base refusal: I despise them. Think not I mean to search in Italy The fatal grandeur which I sacrificed To Titus' love, and in another's arms Lament the weakness which I felt for thee; My fate's determined: learn, proud Roman, thou Whose savage virtue rises but to oppress A helpless woman, coward, when I ask Thy aid, and only valiant to destroy me, Fickle and wavering in thy faith, of me Learn to fulfill thy vows; thou shalt behold A Woman, in thy eyes however contemned, However despised, unshaken in her purpose, And by her firmness see how much she loved thee. Titus, beneath these walls, the reverend seat Of my great ancestors, which thou defendest Against their rightful lord; this fatal spot Where thou hast dared to insult and to betray me; Where first thy faithless vows deceived me; there, Even there, by all the gods who store up vengeance For perjured men, I swear to thee, O Titus, This arm, more just than thine, and more resolved, Shall punish soon my fond credulity, And wash out all my injuries in my blood: I go—

**Titus:** No, Tullia, hear and then condemn me; You shall be satisfied; I fly to please you, Yet shudder at it: I am still more wretched, Because my guilty soul has no excuse, No poor delusion left. I have not even The joy of self-deceit to soothe my sorrows: No, thou hast conquered, not betrayed me, Tullia; I loathe the fatal passion which I feel, And rush on vice, yet know and honor virtue. Hate me, avoid me, leave a guilty wretch Who dies for love, yet hates himself for loving; Nor fears to mix his future fate with thine, Midst crimes, and horrors, perjury, and death.

**Tullia:** You know too well your influence o'er my heart; Mock my fond passion, and insult my love; Yes, Titus, 'tis for thee alone I live, For thee would die: yet, spite of all my love, And all my weakness, death were far more welcome Than the reluctant hand of cruel Titus, Who is ashamed to serve his royal master, And blushes to accept a kingdom from me. The dreadful hour of separation comes, Think on it, Titus, and remember well That Tullia loves, and offers thee a throne. The ambassador expects me; fare thee well, Deliberate and determine: an hour hence Again thou shalt behold me with my father: When I return to these detested walls Know, Titus, I'll return a queen, or perish.

**Titus:** Thou shalt not die: I go—

**Tullia:** Stop, Titus, stop; If thou shouldst follow me, thy life's in danger, Thou'lt be suspected; therefore stay: farewell; Resolve to be my murderer, or my husband.

### SCENE IV.

**Titus:** [Alone.] O Tullia, thou hast conquered, Rome's enslaved: Return to rule o'er her, and o'er my life, Devoted to thee: haste, I fly to crown thee, Or perish in the attempt: the worst of crimes Were to abandon thee. Now, where's Messala? My headstrong passion hath at length worn out His patient friendship; mistress, Romans, friends, All in one fatal day, hath Titus lost.

## SCENE V.

Titus, Messala.

**Titus**: O my Messala, help me in my love, And my revenge: away; haste, follow me.

**Messala**: Command, and I obey: my troops are ready At the Quirinal mount to give us up The gates, and all my gallant friends have sworn To acknowledge Titus as the rightful heir Of Tarquin: lose no time; propitious night Already offers her kind shade to veil Our great design.

**Titus**: The hour approaches: Tullia Will count each minute: Tarquin, after all, Had my first oaths: away, the die is cast. [The lower part of the stage opens and discovers Brutus.] What do I see; my father!

## SCENE VI.

Brutus, Titus, Messala, Lictors.

**Brutus**: Titus, haste, Rome is in danger; thou art all our hope: Secret instructions have been given the senate That Rome will be attacked at dead of night, And I have gained for my beloved Titus The first command, in this extremity Of public danger. Arm thyself, my son, And fly, a second time, to save thy country; Hazard thy life once more in the great cause Of liberty; or victory or death Must crown thy days, and I shall envy thee.

**Titus**: O heaven!

**Brutus**: My son!

**Titus**: To other hands commit The senate's favors, and the fate of Rome.

**Messala**: What strange disorder has possessed his soul!

**Brutus**: Dost thou refuse the proffered glory?

**Titus**: I! Shall I, my lord—

**Brutus**: Ha! doth thy heart still burn With proud resentment of thy fancied wrongs? Is this a time, my son, for fond caprice? Can he who saved his country be unhappy? Immortal honor! will not that suffice Without the consulship? The laws, thou knowest, Refused it, Titus, to thy youth alone, Not to thy merit: think no more of that: Go; I have placed thee in the post of honor; Let tyrants only feel thy indignation; Give Rome thy life; ask nothing in return, But be a hero; be yet more, my son, A Roman: I am hastening to the end Of my short journey; thy victorious hands Must close my eyes; supported by thy virtues, My name shall never die; I shall revive And live once more in Titus: but perhaps It is decreed that I must follow thee; Old age is weak; but I will see thee conquer, Or perish with thee, Rome's avenger still, Free, and without a master.

**Titus**: O Messala!

## SCENE VII.

Brutus, Valerius, Titus, Messala.

**Valerius**: My lord, let all retire.

**Brutus**: [To Titus.] Run, fly, my son—

**Valerius**: Rome is betrayed.

**Brutus**: What do I hear?

**Valerius**: There's treason; We're sold, my lord, the author's yet unknown; But Tarquin's name is echoed through our streets, And worthless Romans talk of yielding to him.

**Brutus**: Ha! would the citizens of Rome be slaves!

**Valerius**: Yes: the perfidious traitors fled from me; I've sent in quest of them: much I suspect Menas and Lælius, the base partisans Of tyranny and kings, the secret foes Of Rome, and ever glad to disunite The senate and the people: if I err not, Protected by Messala, who himself, But for his friendship with the noble Titus, I almost think, has joined them.

**Brutus**: We'll observe Their steps with caution; more cannot be done: The liberty and laws which we defend Forbid that rigor which I fear is needful; But to detain a Roman on suspicions Were to resemble those usurping tyrants Whom we would punish: let us to the people, Awake the fearful, give the virtuous praise, Astonish the perfidious: let the fathers Of Rome and liberty revive the warmth Of Roman courage: who will not be bold When we appear? O rather give us death, Ye gods! than slavery: let the senate follow.

## SCENE VIII.

Brutus, Valerius, Proculus.

**Proculus**: A slave, my lord, desires a private audience.

**Brutus**: At this late hour of night!

**Proculus**: He brings you news, He says, of highest import.

**Brutus**: Ha! perhaps Rome's safety may depend on it: away. [To Proculus.] A moment's loss might hazard all—go thou And seek my son: let the Quirinal gate Be his first care: and may the world confess, When they behold his glorious deeds, the race Of Brutus was decreed to conquer kings.

# ACT V.

SCENE I.

Brutus, Senators, Proculus, Lictors. Vindex (A Slave).

**Brutus**: A little more and Tarquin, armed with vengeance, This night had rushed upon us; Rome had fallen, And freedom sunk beneath the tyrant's power: This subtle statesman, this ambassador, Had opened wide the fatal precipice: Would you believe it, even the sons of Rome United to betray her: false Messala Urged on their furious zeal, and sold his country To this perfidious Aruns; but kind heaven, Still watchful o'er the fate of Rome, preserved us. [Pointing to Vindex.] This slave o'erheard it all; his faithful counsels Awaked my fears, and filled my aged breast With double vigor: I had scized Messala, And hoped by tortures to have wrested from him The names of his associates; but, behold, Surrounded by my lictors, on a sudden He from his bosom drew a poniard forth, Designed no doubt for other purposes, And cried, if you would know Messala's secrets, Look for them here, within this bleeding breast; He who has courage to conspire against you, Can keep the counsel which he gives, and die: Then, as tumultuously they gathered round him, Pierced his false heart, and like a Roman died, Though he had lived unworthy of the name. Already Aruns was beyond the walls Of Rome; our guards pursued him to the camp, Stopped him with Tullia, and ere long will bring The traitor here, when heaven, I trust, will soon Unravel all their dark and deadly purpose. Valerius will detect them: but remember Friends, Romans, countrymen, I charge you all, When ye shall know the names of these vile slaves, These parricides, nor pardon nor indulgence Be shown to friends, to brothers, nay to children; Think on their crimes alone, preserve your faith, For liberty and Rome demand their blood, And he who pardons guilt like theirs, partakes it. [To the slave.] Thou, whose blind destiny and lowly birth Made thee a slave, who shouldst have been a Roman; Thou, by whose generous aid the senate lives, And Rome is safe, receive that liberty Thou hast bestowed; henceforth let nobler thoughts Inspire thy soul; be equal to my sons, The dread of tyrants, the delight of Rome. But whence this tumult? Hark!

**Proculus**: The ambassador Is seized, my lord, and they have brought him hither.

**Brutus**: How will he dare—

SCENE II.

Brutus, Senators, Aruns, Lictors.

**Aruns**: How long, insulting Romans, Will you thus violate the sacred rights Of all mankind? How long by faction led Thus in their ministers dishonor kings? Your lictors have with insolence detained me: Is it my master you thus treat with scorn, Or Aruns? Know, my rank respectable In every nation—

**Brutus**: The more sacred that, More guilty thou: talk not of titles here.

**Aruns**: A king's ambassador—

**brutus**: Thou art not one: Thou are a traitor, with a noble name, Emboldened by impunity: for know That, true ambassadors interpret laws, But never break them; serve their king, but ne'er Dishonor him: with them reposed in safety Lie the firm ties of faith 'twixt man and man; And of their holy ministry the fruit Is grateful peace: they are the sacred bonds That knit the sovereigns of the earth together; And, as the friends of all, by all revered. Ask thy own heart if thou art such; thou darest not: But if thy master bade thee learn our laws, Our virtues, and our treasures, we will teach thee Now what Rome is, and what a Roman senate: Will teach thee that this people still respects The law of nations, which thou hast dishonored: The only punishment inflicted on thee, Shall be to see thy vile associates bleed, And tell thy king their folly and their fate. When thou returnest, be sure inform thy friends Of Rome's resentment, and thy own disgrace: Lictors, away with him.

SCENE III.

Brutus, Valerius, Proculus, Senators.

Well, my Valerius, They're seized, I hope, at least you know the traitors: Ha! wherefore is that melancholy gloom Spread o'er thy face, presaging greater ills? Thou tremblest too.

**Valerius**: Remember thou art Brutus.

**Brutus**: Explain thyself.

**Valerius**: I dare not speak it: take [Gives him the tablets.] These tablets, read, and know the guilty.

**Brutus**: Ha! My eyes deceive me; sure it cannot be! O heavy hour! and most unhappy father! My son! Tiberius! pardon me, my friends, Unlooked for misery! Have you seized the traitor?

**Valerius**: My lord, with two of the conspirators, He stood on his defence, and rather chose To die than yield himself a prisoner: close By them he fell all covered o'er with wounds: But O there still remains a tale more dreadful For thee, for Rome, and for us all.

**Brutus**: What is it?

**Valerius**: Once more, my lord, look on that fatal scroll Which Proculus had wrested from Messala.

**Brutus**: I tremble, but I will go on: ha! Titus! [He sinks into the arms of Proculus.]

**Valerius**: Disarmed I found him, wandering in despair And horror, as if conscious of a crime Which he abhorred.

**Brutus**: Return, ye conscript fathers, Straight to the senate; Brutus hath no place Amongst you now: go, pass your judgment on him, Exterminate the guilty race of Brutus; Punish the father in the blood of him Who was my child: I shall not follow you, Or to suspend or mitigate the wrath Of injured Rome.

## SCENE IV.

**Brutus**: [Alone.] Great gods! to your decrees I yield submissive, to the great avengers Of Rome, and of her laws: by you inspired I reared the structure of fair liberty On justice and on truth; and will you now O'erthrow it? will you arm my children's hands Against your own work? Was it not woe enough That fierce Tiberius, blind with furious zeal, Should serve the tyrant, and betray his country? But that my Titus too, the joy of Rome, Who, full of honor, but this very day

Enjoyed a triumph for his victories, Crowned in the capitol by Brutus' hand, Titus, the hope of my declining years, The darling of mankind, that Titus—gods!

## SCENE V.

Brutus, Valerius, Lictors, Attendants.

**Valerius**: My lord, the senate has decreed, yourself Should pass the sentence on your guilty son.

**Brutus**: Myself!

**Valerius**: It must be so.

**Brutus**: Touching the rest, Say, what have they determined?

**Valerius**: All condemned To death; even now perhaps they are no more.

**Brutus**: And has the senate left to my disposal The life of Titus?

**Valerius**: They esteem this honor Due to thy virtues.

**Brutus**: O my country!

**Valerius**: What Must I return in answer to the senate?

**Brutus**: That Brutus knows the value of a favor He sought not, but shall study to deserve. But could my son without resistance yield? Could he—forgive my doubts, but Titus ever Was Rome's best guard, and still I feel I love him.

**Valerius**: Tullia, my lord—

**Brutus**: Well, what of her?

**Valerius**: Confirmed Our just suspicions.

**Brutus**: How!

**Valerius**: Soon as she saw, In her return, the dreadful preparation Of torture for the offenders, at our feet She fell, and soon in agonies expired; The last poor victim of the hated race Of tyrants: doubtless 'twas for her, my lord, Rome was betrayed: I feel a father's grief, And weep for Brutus; but in her last moments This way she turned her eyes, and called on Titus.

**Brutus**: Just gods!

**Valerius**: Thou art his judge, perform thy office, Or strike, or spare; acquit him, or condemn; Rome will approve what Brutus shall determine.

**Brutus**: Lictors, bring Titus hither.

**Valerius**: I retire, And trust thy virtue; my astonished soul Admires and pities thee: I go to tell The senate, naught can equal Brutus' grief But Brutus' firmness.

SCENE VI.

Brutus, Proculus.

**Brutus**: No: the more I think, The less can I believe my son could e'er Conspire with traitors to betray his country: No: he loved Rome too well; too well he loved His father: sure we cannot thus forget Our duty and ourselves in one short day: I cannot think my son was guilty still.

**Proculus**: 'Twas all conducted by Messala; he Perhaps designed to shelter his own crimes Beneath the name of Titus; his accusers Envy his glory, and would fain obscure it.

**Brutus**: O! would to heaven it were so!

**Proculus**: He's thy son, Thy only hope; and innocent or guilty, The senate has to thee resigned his fate: His life is safe whilst in the hands of Brutus; Thou wilt preserve a great man for his country; Thou art a father.

**Brutus**: No: I am Rome's consul.

## SCENE VII.

Brutus, Proculus.

**Titus**: [At the farther end of the stage, guarded by Lictors.]

**Proculus**: He comes.

**Titus**: [Advancing.] 'Tis Brutus: O distressful sight! Open, thou earth, beneath my trembling steps! My lord, permit a son—

**Brutus**: Rash boy, forbear: I was the father of two children once, And loved them both; but one is lost: what sayest thou? Speak, Titus, have I yet a son?

**Titus**: O no: Thou hast not.

**Brutus**: Answer then thy judge, thou shame To Brutus; say, didst thou betray thy country, Give up thy father to a tyrant's power, And break thy solemn vows? Didst thou resolve To do this, Titus?

**Titus**: I resolved on nothing. Filled with a deadly poison that possessed My frantic mind, I did not know myself, Nor do I yet; and my distempered soul, In its wild rage, was for a moment guilty; That moment clothed me with eternal shame, And made me false to what I loved, my country: 'Tis past; and anguish and remorse succeed To avenge their wrongs, and scourge me for the crime. Pronounce my sentence: Rome, that looks upon thee, Wants an example, and demands my life: By my deserved fate she may deter Those of her sons, if any such there be, Who might be tempted to a crime like mine. In death at least thus shall I serve my country; Thus shall my blood, which never till this hour Was stained with guilt, still flow for liberty.

**Brutus**: Unnatural mixture! perfidy and courage; Such horrid crimes with such exalted virtue! With all thy dear-bought laurels on thy brow, What power malignant could inspire thee thus With vile inconstancy?

**Titus**: The thirst of vengeance, Ambition, hatred, madness; all united—

**Brutus**: Go on, unhappy youth.

**Titus**: One error more, And worse than all the rest; one cruel flame; That fired my guilt, and still perhaps augments it, Completed my destruction: to confess it Is double shame, to Rome of little service, And most unworthy of us both: I own it: But I have reached the summit of my guilt, And of my sorrows too: end with my life My crimes, and my despair, my shame and thine. [Kneeling.] But if in battle I have ever traced Thy glorious steps; if I have followed thee, And served my country; if remorse and anguish Already have o'erpaid my crimes; O deign Within thy arms once more to hold a wretch Abandoned and forlorn: O say, at least, "My son, thy father hates thee not": that word Alone my fame and virtue shall restore, And save my memory from the brand of shame. The world will say, when Titus died, a look From you relieved him from his load of grief, And made him full amends for all his sorrows; Spite of his guilt, that still esteemed by thee, He bore thy blessing with him to the grave.

**Brutus**: O Rome! his pangs oppress me: O my country! Proculus, see they lead my son to death. Rise, wretched Titus, thou wert once the hope Of my old age, my best support; embrace Thy father who condemned thee; 'twas his duty. Were he not Brutus, he had pardoned thee; Believe my tears that trickle down thy cheeks Whilst I am speaking to thee: O my Titus, Let nobler courage than thy father shows Support thee in thy death; my son, farewell: Let no unmanly tears disgrace thy fall, But be a Roman still, and let thy country, That knows thy worth, admire while she destroys thee.

**Titus**: Farewell: I go to death; in that at least Titus once more shall emulate his father.

### SCENE VIII.

Brutus, Proculus.

**Proculus**: My lord, the senate, with sincerest grief, And shuddering at the dreadful stroke—

**Brutus**: No more: Ye know not Brutus who condole with him At such a time: Rome only is my care; I feel but for my country: we must guard Against more danger: they're in arms again: Away: let Rome in this disastrous hour Supply the place of him whom I have lost For her, and let me finish my sad days, As Titus should have done, in Rome's defence.

SCENE the LAST.

**Brutus**, Proculus, a Senator.

**Senator**: My lord—

**Brutus**: My son is dead?

**Senator**: 'Tis so: these eyes—

**Brutus**: Thank heaven! Rome's free; and I am satisfied.

### End

www.ingramcontent.com/pod-product-compliance
Lightning Source LLC
Chambersburg PA
CBHW031438040426
42444CB00006B/868